ANSWER IT!

NANCY DUFRESNE

DUFRESNE MINISTRIES
PUBLICATIONS

Answer It!
ISBN: 978-0-940763-43-2
Copyright © 2018, 2022, 2023 by Dufresne Ministries

Published by:
Dufresne Ministries Publications
P.O. Box 1010
Murrieta, CA 92564
www.dufresneministries.org

1-5000   2-3000   3-5000

Unless otherwise indicated, all Scriptural quotations are from the *King James Version* of the Bible.

Scripture quotations marked AMPC are taken from the *Amplified® Bible, Classic Edition (AMPC)*, Copyright © 1954, 1958, 1962, 1964, 1965, 1987 by The Lockman Foundation. Used by permission. www.Lockman.org

Scripture quotations marked NIV are taken from the *Holy Bible, New International Version®*, NIV® Copyright ©1973, 1978, 1984, 2011 by Biblica, Inc.® Used by permission. All rights reserved worldwide. www.biblica.com

Cover design: Nancy Dufresne & Grant Dufresne

Nancy Dufresne's photo © Dufresne Ministries

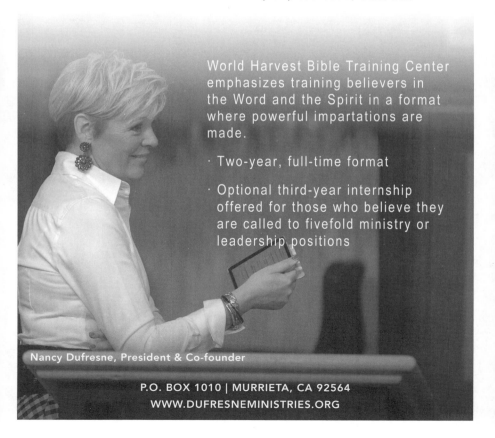

Books by Nancy Dufresne

Daily Healing Bread From God's Table

His Presence Shall Be My Dwelling Place

The Healer Divine

Victory in the Name

*There Came a Sound From Heaven:
The Life Story of Dr. Ed Dufresne*

Visitations From God

Responding to the Holy Spirit

God: The Revealer of Secrets

A Supernatural Prayer Life

Causes

I Have A Supply

*Fit for the Master's Use:
A Handbook for Raising Godly Children*

A Sound, Disciplined Mind

Knowing Your Measure of Faith

The Greatness of God's Power

Peace: Living Free From Worry

Following the Holy Spirit

An Apostle of the Anointing:
A Biography of Dr. Ed Dufresne

Victory Over Grief & Sorrow

The Price of the Double Portion Anointing

Worship

Love: The Great Quest

Books in Spanish

Pan Diario de Sanidad de la Mesa de Dios
(Spanish edition of *Daily Healing Bread*)

Contents

Preface

The truths and revelations I share with you in this book are so precious and dear to me because they were my answer and exit door out of some difficult seasons of tests that I faced. It was in these tests that I learned revelations and gained skill in using those revelations against the strategies of the enemy.

I encourage you to read the entire book, for each chapter holds different revelations that will help you see and become skillful with your all-conquering victory so that you live in total peace and live days of Heaven on the earth.

Introduction

The truths in this book are more clear to you when you understand the authority and victory that belong to every child of God.

Colossians 2:15 tells us that Jesus spoiled, defeated, and stripped Satan in His total conquest and victory over him. Satan is a defeated foe. Jesus defeated Satan on our behalf, then handed us that victory, so Satan no longer dominates us.

Colossians 1:13 tells us, *"Who HATH delivered us from the power of darkness, and hath translated us into the kingdom of his dear Son."* God has *already* delivered us from every flow of Satan's kingdom, the kingdom of darkness.

Jesus stated, *"The thief cometh not, but for to steal, and to kill, and to destroy: I am come that they might have life, and that they might have it more abundantly"* (John 10:10).

Anything that steals, kills, and destroys is of Satan; that's the flow of the kingdom of darkness. And we are already delivered from that kingdom! We belong to a *new* Kingdom now – the Kingdom of His dear Son!

As believers, we need to understand that we are *already* delivered from every evil thing that comes from the kingdom of darkness and refuse to allow the enemy to steal from us.

No, we're not trying to *get* free – we are already delivered! And because we are, we *refuse* to allow the devil to steal from us!

In every encounter with the enemy, we are to face him with the knowledge and mindset that he is already a defeated foe. We are not to ever try to fight Satan to win the victory Jesus already won for us. We are simply to *enforce* the victory Jesus made ours.

The devil doesn't want you to know this great truth. When believers know and understand this and exercise their authority over him, all of the devil's attempts against them are unsuccessful.

Hosea 4:6 informs us, *"My people are destroyed for lack of knowledge...."* When believers are ignorant of what belongs to them, the enemy is able to take advantage of them.

When Christians have the mindset that they are *trying* to get free, they don't yet understand this great truth in Colossians 1:13, that we are already free – we have already been delivered from everything of Satan's kingdom.

Christ has already made us free, but it is up to us to enforce our freedom and victory. We aren't trying to get free – Satan is trying to steal our freedom from us through fear, worry, doubt, sickness, lack, and everything else that steals – but we refuse and resist him, standing our ground against him. Tell all opposition and temptations, "I am already free from you! So you go from me, in Jesus' Name!"

You will enjoy the freedom God made yours as you stand your ground against all opposition and ANSWER IT!

Chapter 1

Talk to Things

One of the most important things that every believer must learn in their life of faith is how to answer opposition. Many times, some are hoping that the devil, opposition, and hindrances will just stop or simply leave them alone, but real faith answers that which opposes it.

Our usefulness to God grows as we become more skillful at answering opposition and at standing our ground against all enemies and circumstances.

When we look at Jesus' earthly ministry, we see our example of what real faith does when faced with opposition, enemies, and circumstances.

> **MARK 11:12-14**
> **12 And on the morrow, when they were come from Bethany, he** (Jesus) **was hungry:**
> **13 And seeing a fig tree afar off having leaves, he came, if haply he might find any thing thereon: and when he came to it, he FOUND NOTHING but leaves; for the time of figs was not yet.**
> **14 And Jesus ANSWERED and said unto it, No man eat fruit of thee hereafter for ever. And his disciples heard it.**

Notice that Jesus needed something. Needs showed up in Jesus' life just like they show up in ours.

When He faced a need of food, He came up to a tree that looked like it would have fruit on it, but when He got there, He found nothing! Have you ever faced a need, but found nothing? What do you do when you come up to nothing? What did Jesus do?

Verse 14 tells us what Jesus did – He answered it! Jesus answered the tree! Jesus talked to things!

By not bearing any fruit, that tree was talking to Him, so He answered it! In His need, it said there was no supply for Him, so He answered it.

Keep Moving On

What did Jesus do after He answered the tree? The next verse (vs. 15) says that they came to Jerusalem. So, after He talked to the tree, He didn't stand there to see if what He said would work or if anything had changed. No, He just answered it and then kept going.

That's such an important action to faith – answer things, then just keep going. Don't stop, don't slow your pace, don't linger behind to see if what you said worked. Answer things that need to change, then keep going on your way.

This is a mistake that many make in facing opposition. They answer their problem with the Word of God, then they keep their eye on the situation to see if it changes, or at least gets better. They make the mistake of holding their attention on the problem.

Jesus just spoke to the tree and then walked off! He didn't let His attention stay on that tree to see if it changed. He didn't answer the tree and then pause to see if it worked.

Some will answer the symptoms in their body, then pause to see if it worked. Did the pain leave? Did the condition change? No, Jesus didn't do that. He didn't let His attention linger on the tree. He spoke to it and then walked off, continuing on His journey. That's what faith does – it answers opposition, then turns and walks off and resumes living – moving on to the next thing without allowing its attention to linger on the opposition.

Nothing appeared to be different about the tree immediately after Jesus spoke to it. But He didn't keep His eye on the tree to see if it worked; He just went on His way.

The power of God meets faith, so Jesus left His words of faith with that tree, and the power in those "faith words" did the work. When something in your life needs changing, speak words of faith and let the power in those words do the work. That's the power of faith!

How Faith Works

In fact, Jesus never brought up the tree again. It was Peter who drew everyone's attention to it the next day as they passed by the same place.

MARK 11:20-26

20 And in the morning, as they passed by, they saw the fig tree dried up from the roots.

21 And Peter calling to remembrance saith unto him, Master, behold, the fig tree which thou cursedst is withered away.

22 And Jesus answering saith unto them, Have faith in God (Hebrew – Have the faith of God).

23 For verily I say unto you, That whosoever shall say unto this mountain, Be thou removed, and be thou cast into the sea; and shall not doubt in his heart, but shall believe that those things which he saith shall come to pass; he shall have whatsoever he saith.

24 Therefore I say unto you, What things soever ye desire, when ye pray, believe that ye receive them, and ye shall have them.

25 And when ye stand praying, forgive, if ye have ought against any: that your Father also which is in heaven may forgive you your trespasses.

26 But if ye do not forgive, neither will your Father which is in heaven forgive your trespasses.

In these verses, Jesus tells His disciples how the faith of God works. He tells them how He was able to speak to the tree and it obeyed Him.

MARK 11:23

For verily I say unto you, That whosoever shall say unto this mountain, Be thou removed, and be thou cast into the sea; and shall not doubt in his heart, but shall believe that those things

**which he saith shall come to pass; he shall have
whatsoever he saith.**

In verse 23, Jesus is simply saying that things will obey
you – so talk to them! If things are not as they should be,
talk to them! When things are not as they should be, they are
saying something to you – answer them! Don't allow them
to remain as they are – answer them! The God-kind of faith
answers things!

We are to believe that when we answer them, they
must obey us – they must obey words of faith, because those
words contain the power to bring it to pass! The last phrase
of verse 23 says, *"...he SHALL have whatsoever he saith."*
Don't stand around with your attention fixed on what you
just spoke to to see if it worked. If you really believe in your
heart that something happened at the time that you spoke
to it, regardless of whether you see any change or not, you'll
just walk off and journey on to the next thing. Faith people
keep moving ahead, trusting in God's power that's in their
words of faith to do the work.

Forgive

In Jesus explaining how the faith of God works, He also
told us in verses 25 & 26 one thing that will keep our faith
from working – and that's unforgiveness. Unforgiveness is
a faith-killer! We can't allow any unforgiveness in our life
toward anyone if our faith is to work.

You're Authorized

When faced with something that needs changing, many sit back and wait for God to do something on their behalf, but Jesus didn't wait for God to do something regarding that tree – HE did something! He initiated the change that He desired by answering that tree.

If you need or want something to change, YOU are the one who has to initiate it by talking to it. No, you're not the one who does the work – God does the work. But YOU must initiate the change that you want by talking to it, then God's power will go to work on your behalf. God will back you up!

Do we have scripture for this? Certainly! Matthew tells us what Jesus said.

> **MATTHEW 16:19**
> **And I will give unto thee the keys of the kingdom of heaven: and whatsoever THOU shalt bind on earth shall be bound in heaven; and whatsoever THOU shalt loose on earth shall be loosed in heaven.**

Notice in this verse that something has to be done on the earth before Heaven takes action. Someone on the earth has to bind or loose something before Heaven does something. This verse shows us that Heaven will back us up. When we either forbid or invite something on the earth to happen, it must be in line with the Word of God. When it is, Heaven backs us up with power.

In fact, there are things that God wants for the earth that will never happen or stop happening until someone on the earth binds or looses them.

Why is that? Jesus told us why in the verse that we just read, *"And I will give unto THEE the keys of the kingdom of heaven...."* We are the ones with the keys. What do these keys do? This verse tells us. They give US the authority to bind and loose things on the earth – to forbid or permit things to happen on the earth.

Let me give you an example of this. If I drive my car to a restaurant that has valet service to park my car, I have to give them my key. If I give them my key to park the car, then I don't have it anymore, and I can't drive the car again until I get my key back, even though I'm the owner of the car.

 Jesus is saying in Matthew 16:19 that that's what He did – He gave the keys of binding and loosing things on the earth to us, so He doesn't have them anymore – we do! Even though He's the One who defeated the devil for us, He transferred the authority to us – we now have the keys of dominion on the earth over our life. If we don't use the keys, He can't! He doesn't have them anymore – we do!

So many people wonder why God doesn't do certain things on this earth, or why He permits certain things to happen. They don't understand that He gave the authority back to man, so man is the one who has to initiate any needed changes on the earth, and when he does, then God will back us up by His power to bring it to pass.

The majority of the things that we receive from God are initiated by us – not by God. We are the ones with the authority to initiate what we need, and if we don't initiate them with our authority, we won't receive what we need.

God already initiated our help by giving us that authority, but in the face of needs, we are the ones that are authorized to initiate the exercising of that authority.

Religious thinking struggles with this truth, but we must go back to the Word and see what the Word says. We can't just go by religious thinking.

It Doesn't Matter What You "Feel" Like

If something in your life needs changing, answer it! If symptoms try to attach themselves to your body, answer them. If lack tries to hinder your finances, answer it! Things will obey you – talk to them! The keys of authority and dominion are yours – use them!

Someone may say, "I don't feel like that works for me. I know it works for others, but not for me."

When a policeman is issued a badge, the badge represents the authority of a city. When that policeman is faced with a lawbreaker, a violator, all he has to do is hold up the badge that was issued to him by the police department, and his authority will work for him. It's not his own authority he's using; he's exercising the authority given to him by a higher power than himself – the authority of a city.

Even if that policeman wakes up one morning and doesn't feel well physically and has little physical strength, his badge of authority didn't lose any strength. Him not feeling well doesn't diminish one degree of power that that badge gives him. It will still work to its full authority for him.

Likewise, even if you don't "feel" strong, or you don't "feel" very spiritual, your feelings don't diminish in the least degree the authority and dominion that Jesus has given you. No matter what you "feel" like, your authority still works – use it to change your situation, the things in your life, and things in the earth.

Come, Go, Do This

Do you remember the passage involving the officer in the Roman army? Let's look at it in the book of Matthew.

MATTHEW 8:5-10
5   And when Jesus was entered into Capernaum, there came unto him a centurion, beseeching him,
6   And saying, Lord, my servant lieth at home sick of the palsy, grievously tormented.
7   And Jesus saith unto him, I will come and heal him.
8   The centurion answered and said, Lord, I am not worthy that thou shouldest come under my roof: but speak the word only, and my servant shall be healed.
9   For I am a man under authority, having soldiers under me: and I say to this man, Go, and

he goeth; and to another, Come, and he cometh; and to my servant, Do this, and he doeth it. 10 When Jesus heard it, he marvelled, and said to them that followed, Verily I say unto you, I have not found so great faith, no, not in Israel.

Jesus placed on this centurion's life another badge – a badge of great faith. He declared about this officer that he had a greatness of faith that He hadn't seen among any others in Israel.

What did his great faith look like? What did he do to express great faith? This centurion answered things – he talked to things! He told soldiers under his authority to, "Go, come, and do this," and they obeyed him. He realized that Jesus' words would accomplish the same thing.

When he told Jesus of his servant's condition, Jesus said that He would go to the centurion's house and deal with it. But the officer had faith enough to say, "You don't need to come to my house; Your word is enough for this. Just speak – that sickness will obey You."

We now have that same authority that Jesus exercised. What will that authority work for us? The same thing that the centurion's authority worked for him. He would say, "Come, go, or do this." We need some things to COME in our life – we can tell them to come. We need some things to GO from our life – we can tell them to go. We need some things to BE DONE in our life – we can tell them to be done.

Great faith will use its authority. Great faith will talk to things – "Come, go, be done!"

Chapter 2

Answer Specifically

To have strong faith and to live a life of success, you not only need to know how to talk to God, but you also need to know how to talk to the devil. We talk to God in fellowship, but we talk to the devil in authority – exercising our authority over him.

LUKE 4:1-14
1   And Jesus being full of the Holy Ghost returned from Jordan, and was led by the Spirit into the wilderness,
2   Being forty days tempted of the devil. And in those days he did eat nothing: and when they were ended, he afterward hungered.
3   And the devil said unto him, If thou be the Son of God, command this stone that it be made bread.
4   And Jesus answered him, saying, It is written, That man shall not live by bread alone, but by every word of God.
5   And the devil, taking him up into an high mountain, shewed unto him all the kingdoms of the world in a moment of time.
6   And the devil said unto him, All this power will I give thee, and the glory of them: for that

is delivered unto me; and to whomsoever I will I give it.

7   If thou therefore wilt worship me, all shall be thine.

8   And Jesus answered and said unto him, Get thee behind me, Satan: for it is written, Thou shalt worship the Lord thy God, and him only shalt thou serve.

9   And he brought him to Jerusalem, and set him on a pinnacle of the temple, and said unto him, If thou be the Son of God, cast thyself down from hence:

10 For it is written, He shall give his angels charge over thee, to keep thee:

11 And in their hands they shall bear thee up, lest at any time thou dash thy foot against a stone.

12 And Jesus answering said unto him, It is said, Thou shalt not tempt the Lord thy God.

13 And when the devil had ended all the temptation, he departed from him for a season.

14 And Jesus returned in the power of the Spirit into Galilee....

Notice the three recorded temptations that Jesus faced. The first one was in verses 3 & 4. *"And the devil SAID unto him, If thou be the Son of God, command this stone that it be made bread. And Jesus ANSWERED him, saying, It is written, That man shall not live by bread alone, but by every word of God."*

I want you to see that Jesus answered the devil *specifically*, in line with the temptation that Satan brought.

When Satan challenged Jesus to turn the stone into bread, Jesus didn't answer with, "I'm anointed," or, "I'm the Son of God," or, "God loves Me." All of those things were true, but they were not the answer to give to Satan's temptation.

When the enemy threatens or tempts you in a particular direction, you must answer specifically in line with the temptation – that's what Jesus did.

Satan tempted Him regarding bread, and Jesus answered him regarding bread – that man shall not live by bread alone, but by every word of God.

On the second temptation, Satan offered Him the power, the glory, and the riches of the kingdoms of this world if Jesus would only worship him. He was offering Jesus a crossless crown and a bloodless glory.

Jesus would have restored to Him the glory and virtue that He had laid aside to be born a man, but only through carrying out His Father's plan – through the avenue of the Cross, through taking upon Himself the sin and sickness of humanity, through going to hell in man's place and utterly defeating and stripping Satan and the demon spirits of all power and authority, and by then being raised to His rightful place, seated at the right hand of His Father; thereby, bringing many sons into glory.

Satan offered Him fleeting power and glory for Himself alone, but instead, Jesus won it for all mankind for all of eternity.

Satan offered Jesus this world's power and glory if He would worship him, and Jesus again answered specifically, in line with the temptation. *"...Thou shalt worship the Lord thy God, and him only shalt thou serve."*

On the third recorded temptation, Satan tempted Jesus to throw Himself off the pinnacle of the Temple, saying that the angels would rescue Him. But again, Jesus answered this temptation specifically, in line with what Satan said. *"...Thou shalt not tempt the Lord thy God."*

Specific Answers

When we answer the enemy's threats, temptations, and oppositions, it's important that we answer them *specifically*, not *generally*.

If the devil were to threaten you with the thought that you're going to lose your house, answering generally with, "The Lord loves me," is the wrong answer. It's true that the Lord loves you, but you have to answer in line with the threat.

Your answer should be, "I'll never lose my house, for the Word says that my God shall supply all my need! I always have a supply for every need of my home!"

Your victory calls for *specific* answers to the devil's threats – not *general* ones!

Every person moving with God's plan will face tests and temptations from the devil, but Jesus demonstrated to us that we are to answer each one. Jesus answered with the Word. Answer every test with what the Word says.

God's Wisdom in a Test

When faced with a need or a test, if you don't know the *specific* answer to give, ask God for His wisdom. God's wisdom is His mind and thoughts. Proverbs 4:7 & 8 tells us, *"Wisdom is the principal thing; therefore get wisdom: and with all thy getting get understanding. Exalt her, and she shall promote thee...."* Find out *His* thinking and what *He* says pertaining to your situation. God's wisdom will promote us. Having God's wisdom will promote us into God's best and into God's plan for our life, but God's wisdom will also promote us out of tests.

If you are doing all you know to do and nothing is changing, you need God's wisdom – ask Him.

> **JAMES 1:2, 5 & 6**
> **2   My brethren, count it all joy when ye fall into divers temptations;**
> **5   If any of you lack wisdom, let him ask of God, that giveth to all men liberally, and upbraideth not; and it shall be given him.**
> **6   But let him ask in faith, nothing wavering....**

This passage starts off talking about tests and temptations we're facing. Then it tells us what to do if we lack wisdom in the face of tests – ask God! Wisdom isn't given automatically – we must *ask* – ask in faith, *expecting* an answer!

On one occasion, there was a threat the enemy kept making against my mind. I didn't know the *specific* answer to it, so I would answer it *generally* with the truths of the

Word, and it would just stand off. But after a few weeks, that same opposition would return. I would again give a *general* answer, and it would again back off, but it didn't leave.

The last time it came, God said to me, "Ask Me about that opposition." I hadn't talked to God about it because I didn't want to touch that threat in my thought life – I didn't want to turn it over in my mind. But when God told me to ask Him about it, I did. He told me *why* it was coming. God gave me the specific answer to give to that threat, and when I answered that threat *specifically*, that devil left and didn't come back. The enemy's strategy failed because the wisdom of God came.

Colossians 1:9 reads, *"...We continually ask God to fill you with the knowledge of his will through all THE WISDOM AND UNDERSTANDING THAT THE SPIRIT GIVES"* (NIV). The Spirit of God will reveal to us God's wisdom for our situation.

When we resist an attack, but it keeps recurring, it's because we aren't yet giving the right *specific* answer. We need God's wisdom. Specifics given by the Spirit of God are the wisdom of God for your need, and wisdom is the principal thing that gets results every time when we add our faith and obedience to it.

Wisdom Is Specific

The book of Mark tells us about how Jesus ministered to the madman of Gadara. *"But when he saw Jesus afar off, he ran and worshipped him, And cried with a loud voice, and said, What have I to do with thee, Jesus, thou Son of the most high God? I adjure thee by God, that thou torment me not. For he said unto him, Come out of the man, thou unclean spirit. And he asked him, What is thy name? And he answered, saying, My name is Legion: for we are many"* (Mark 5:6-9).

Notice, Jesus had commanded the devil to come out once, but he didn't, so Jesus asked him his name. When Jesus called the demon out by name, the *specific* name, the demons came out – He got results.

This shows us that when faced with opposition, we sometimes need to answer opposition with more *specific* answers and not just *general* answers if we are to get results.

If you are having to deal with the same opposition repeatedly, you need God's wisdom to know the *specific* answer to give.

We are to live "days of Heaven upon the earth" (Deut. 11:21). We aren't to live troubled and harassed by ongoing opposition. Troubling is not to last; it is not to be a way of life for the believer.

Ask God for His wisdom, which is your *specific* answer to the test – then when standing on that Word, you'll get results!

Demonstrate Your Victory

Luke 4:1 tells us that *"...Jesus being FULL of the Holy Ghost...was LED by the Spirit into the wilderness."* The Spirit didn't lead Him to that place of temptation to "see who would win." Rather, the Spirit led Him there to prove Jesus' consecration to God's plan, to exercise His mastery over the devil, and to demonstrate Himself as the Victor.

Jesus wasn't just the Victor upon His exit from the 40 days in the wilderness. Jesus was the Victor going in, during, and when exiting that wilderness.

Luke 4 spells out three of the temptations that Jesus encountered against His spirit, His soul, and His body, but Luke 4:2 reads, *"Being forty days tempted of the devil."* For the entire 40 days, He was being tempted. We could call this a season of temptations.

On day one of the temptations, you know that Jesus answered right, but just because He answered right didn't mean that the temptations stopped. Even after He answered right, the devil kept talking. He answered right on day two, day three, day four, and every day thereafter.

Just because you answer right doesn't mean that the devil will quit talking and the temptations will stop. And just because temptations continue doesn't mean that you're answering wrong, and it doesn't mean that the Word isn't working or that your faith isn't working.

No matter how long the season of temptation lasts, keep answering every temptation right. Once the devil's cycle of temptation is complete, it will pass. You can't keep the devil from talking, but you must answer him specifically with the Word every time.

Remember, you're not only the victor when you pass a test successfully, but you are the victor during the test, for Jesus won the victory for us and handed it to us. Just keep demonstrating the victory that is already yours!

The Last Word Stands

When I was growing up, my mother made it clear to us four kids that the last word was hers, not ours. When she said something, if we tried to argue with her or get the last word, trouble was headed our way.

Why did mother not let us have the last word? Because she knew that the last word stands.

In His earthly ministry, Jesus never let Satan have the last word. Jesus always answered the devil and showed Himself the Victor.

It's always a shock to me when I'm out in public and see a child arguing and talking back to a parent. That parent doesn't know that the authority over the child is theirs and that the last word is theirs. When a child gets the last word, that parent has laid down their authority to a child. What a sad day when a parent lays down their authority to a child, giving them the last word.

Likewise, when we fail to answer the threats, accusations, symptoms, harassments, lack, and opposition that the devil brings, we are doing what that parent does with their child –

laying down our authority to the one who has no authority over us – and then the devil gets the last word in that situation.

No matter how long a parent lays down their authority to a child, once they realize what they are doing, they are still authorized to take it up again at any time and start exercising it. Their authority will still work.

Likewise, when a Christian sees that they have been laying down their authority to the devil, they can again take it back up, and their authority will still work for them.

Jesus has given us the authority over all the power of the enemy. The last word is ours – use it! Everything the enemy says or tries to do against you is to be answered – every wrong, troubling, fearful thought, and every doubt or accusation is to be answered.

You Must "Answer" For Yourself

Each Christian must learn that every thought that comes *to* you didn't come *from* you. You must learn to recognize when the enemy is talking to your mind and answer it! Any thought that robs you of joy and peace is to be cast down by answering it (2 Cor. 10:5).

There are Christians who are sick, depressed, harassed, fearful, tormented, and living in lack because they have not learned to answer these things.

No one else can do your "answering" for you. Ministers and other believers can instruct and encourage you in these things, but every person will have to learn to answer for themselves when circumstances and oppositions arise to try to steal from them.

A husband can't answer for his wife, a wife can't answer for her husband, a pastor can't answer for his congregation members – every believer must learn to answer for himself.

While children are young, they are under their parents' faith and authority, but as children grow up, they will have to learn how to answer the devil for themselves.

As ministers, my husband and I taught our sons that they not only have to have their own fellowship with God, but we also taught them that they must learn to answer the devil for themselves.

Ministers' children must learn to answer the devil, circumstances, oppositions, and tests for themselves. They can't assume that just because their parents are ministers and know how to overcome the enemy that that's enough for them, too. They must develop their own faith and fellowship with God and learn to answer the devil for themselves. The parents need to teach their kids that they have the authority to answer the enemy.

No one can succeed just because their pastor, spouse, parent, or loved one knows how to answer the devil; each one must learn to answer the devil for themselves.

"Oh, It's Just You!"

One of my favorite stories demonstrating this is the time that Smith Wigglesworth, an English preacher of the early 1900s, was awakened one night when he sensed an evil presence in the room. He awakened to find Satan sitting on his bed in manifested form. Brother Wigglesworth saw him and answered, "Oh, it's just you!" Then he rolled over and went back to sleep. He was completely unafraid and unimpressed at Satan's presence. What a masterful answer Wigglesworth gave!

When we understand our authority and complete dominion over the devil, we too are to show ourselves masterful, unafraid, and unimpressed by Satan's threats and devices.

On one occasion, Smith Wigglesworth also stated, "Shout, 'Get thee behind me, Satan,' and you will have the best time on earth. Whisper it, and you won't."

Chapter 3

Victory in Three Arenas

There are three arenas that we must deal with, and Jesus has given us victory over all three – the flesh, the world, and the devil. Our authority works regarding each of these, and we must become skillful with answering them when they try to get out of place.

#1 – Victory Over the Flesh

Bad habits, addictions, and temptations of the flesh are able to be overcome as we take our stand on the Word and answer these things.

When old bad habits or addictions try to resurface, they can be successfully resisted as you answer them. You don't have to allow them to trouble and harass you or take your life off course. Answer them with the Word and stand your ground against them, no matter how long they persist – outlast them by answering them. Tell them, "No, in Jesus' Name!"

Matthew 26:41 records what Jesus instructed His disciples: *"Watch and PRAY, that ye enter not into temptation: the spirit indeed is willing, but the flesh is weak."*

As you spend time with God in prayer, your spirit will be strengthened and fortified. *"But they that wait upon the Lord shall renew their strength..."* (Is. 40:31). You wait upon the Lord through prayer and through spending time worshipping Him. From that strength in your spirit, you can successfully resist addictions, bad habits, and all opposition, as you resist those temptations with the Word of God, refusing to yield to them.

When you set your own will in agreement with God's will, the enemy will try to get you to change your will; he will tempt you to desire something that you know is different than what God wants for you.

In the past, when temptations came to try to get me to change my will to go against God's will, the enemy would try to get me to desire something against God's will. When that temptation would come, I would answer it by saying, "That thought and that desire is not mine. I resist that. That is not God's will for me; therefore it is not my will. That is not pleasing to God; therefore, it's not pleasing to me, so you go from me in Jesus' Name!"

Every time a wrong desire or thought would come, I recognized that it was trying to get my will out of agreement with God's will, so I would refuse by answering it. Then I would refuse to entertain that mentally. I would answer it every time it came to me.

Years ago, God said to me, "When a believer succumbs to sin, some may say, 'Well, that sin caused them to fall.' No, it wasn't the sin. It was their failure to start their day with Me. If they would have started their day with Me (in the Word and prayer), they would have been strengthened to take their stand against that temptation."

Romans 6:14 reads, *"For sin SHALL NOT have dominion over you...."* Verse 18 tells us, *"Being then made FREE FROM SIN, ye became the servants of righteousness."* Jesus freed us from the power of sin. It has no power over us; it cannot dominate us and lord over us, for we have a new Lord.

Romans 6:13 instructs us how to keep from being dominated by the flesh and by sin. *"Neither yield ye your members as instruments of unrighteousness unto sin: but YIELD yourselves unto God...."* Refuse to yield to sin and temptations. Answer every temptation to sin, "I am free from you! You have no power over me, and I refuse to yield to you!"

#2 – Victory Over the World

The flow of this world is all around us, but we don't have to allow that flow to govern or dominate us or our families. When the things of the world try to gain an entrance into your life, your family, or your home, you're authorized to answer them with the Word.

Fear, doubt, grief, sorrow, depression, sickness, lack, and defeat are found in the life of those without God in this world, but they don't belong in our life. We are IN the world, but we are not OF the world (John 15:19; John 17:14).

When these things try to gain entrance, we are authorized to answer them! Forbid their entrance into your life and home – they don't belong to you!

#3 – Victory Over the Devil

"And having spoiled principalities and powers, he (Jesus) *made a shew of them openly, triumphing over them in it"* (Col. 2:15).

Jesus told you, *"Behold, I give unto you power* (authority) *to tread on serpents and scorpions, and over ALL the power of the enemy: and nothing shall by any means hurt you"* (Luke 10:19). No means or strategy the devil launches or tries to work against you will be successful as you exercise the authority Jesus gave you. How do you exercise it? Answer it!

When the devil attacks you, your life, your family, your home, your marriage, your business, your mind, your body, or anything of yours, victory is sure as you answer him.

You are a spirit, you live in a body, and you have a mind.

Someone may ask, "Can a Christian have a devil?" No, not in his spirit, because the Holy Spirit dwells in the spirit of every Christian. The Holy Spirit and the devil cannot dwell together in the same temple.

But a devil can get in the body of a Christian, causing sickness and disease. (Not all sickness and disease means someone has a devil in their body, although sickness and disease are indirectly caused by the devil.)

A devil can also get into the mind of a Christian. How? By them listening to the devil and entertaining the thoughts he gives.

You can't keep the devil from talking to you, but you can certainly have something to say to him when he does. Answer him!

Recognize that every thought that comes to your mind doesn't originate with your mind. The devil will suggest a thought to your mind hoping you will accept it as your own thought. But recognize when a thought is not in line with the Word of God, and resist it by answering it. Refuse to accept it or entertain it by answering it. No matter how many times that thought comes to you, be it long or short, answer it – outlast it. Victory over the devil belongs to you! Don't listen to him – rather, make him listen to you as you answer him!

Chapter 4

Put It Back!

Second Corinthians 4:8 & 9 lists some of the Apostle Paul's persecutions. As he tells of some of the trials he faced, notice that he answered each one. *"We are troubled on every side...."* Then his answer to it, *"...yet not distressed; we are perplexed...."* His answer, *"...but not in despair; Persecuted...."* He answers it, *"...but not forsaken; cast down...."* Paul's answer, *"...but not destroyed."*

Yes, Paul was opposed much, but he understood that every opposition was to be answered. It's not enough to answer some or even most oppositions, but each one, as Paul demonstrated.

Bitten by Devils

God sent a missionary to Manila, Philippines, in the 1950s, where he had a mighty revival. The revival started with a miracle for a teenage girl. The girl had been orphaned at a very young age and was drawn into prostitution as a way to survive on the streets. At the age of 17, she was arrested and thrown into prison. While there, bite marks would appear on her body, and she would scream, appearing to fight against some unseen force.

While in prison, a doctor and prison guard died when she spoke a curse on them. The city officials were frightened by the dramatic events surrounding this girl.

When they implored on public radio for someone to come help this girl, God spoke to the missionary to go to the prison and cast the devil out of her.

When he went into her cell, the demon that possessed her spoke through her and cursed the missionary by name. Although the girl didn't speak English, that demon that spoke through her used English.

When that demon cursed the missionary and his family, the missionary answered each curse specifically against his family, listing the honorable attributes of his parents.

The demon then cursed God, using foul, profane language. Then the missionary answered that curse specifically, listing the conquering attributes of the greatness of God.

The demon then cursed the Name of Jesus with profane language. The missionary again answered, listing specifically the conquering attributes of the mighty Name of Jesus.

After that, the demon, using profanity, started cursing the Blood of Jesus. Again, with great boldness, the missionary listed specifically all of the redeeming, life-giving attributes of the Blood of Jesus.

After answering the demon's curses, the missionary then cast the demon out of the girl, and she was gloriously set free.

After the missionary ministered to her, he told her that if that demon tried to come back, she was to answer that demon and forbid him entrance back into her life in the Name of Jesus.

The prison officials saw the deliverance and glorious change in the girl and scheduled her release for the next day.

However, that night, that demon once again came into her prison cell, but the missionary had taught her what to do — so she answered it! She refused to allow its entrance back into her in the Name of Jesus, and she walked out of prison completely free. Although she had only gotten saved that day and was a baby Christian, her authority over the devil was complete and total. As she exercised her authority, it worked!

The missionary placed her in the home of a Christian couple, and several years later, she became the wife of a pastor.

The mayor was so grateful for the missionary's ministry to the girl that he permitted the missionary to have a mass open-air meeting for the next two weeks on prime property in the heart of Manila, where 100,000 people were born again.

Because the missionary knew how to answer the devil, a revival came to the Philippines that changed the entire nation.

When the missionary first heard the radio broadcast from the city officials asking for anyone that could help the girl to come to the prison, God spoke to him to go there to set her free. The missionary answered God, "Why don't You send someone else?"

God responded, "I don't have anyone else!" What a sobering statement.

There were hundreds of churches and ministers in Manila. What did God mean when He said that He didn't have anyone else? He didn't have anyone who knew how to answer the devil!

There were, no doubt, many who loved God, but God needed someone who knew how to answer the devil.

If we are to be of great use to God, we too must know how to answer the devil.

When Jesus encountered the devil manifesting through an individual during His earthly ministry, the way He answered was, "Shut up, and come out!"

No, we don't carry on conversations with the devil, but we must learn to recognize when he is operating and answer him whenever and wherever he may be operating.

This missionary was a man who knew his God-given authority and walked boldly in it.

That same authority belongs to you, too! Use it and become skillful with it!

Put It Back!

Another story that this same missionary told of was a time that he was ministering in Java. He was asleep one night as the bed started bouncing wildly up and down from one leg to the other. An evil presence was tangible in the room. The bed bounced so violently that it had moved away from the wall and was now sitting out in the middle of the room. The missionary boldly spoke, telling the evil spirit to get out of the room in the Name of Jesus.

Immediately, the bed stopped moving, and he could sense that the evil presence was no longer in the room.

The missionary began to get out of bed to move it back to the wall, but as he did, he thought, *Why should I be the one to get out of bed to put it back?* Boldly he yelled, "Devil! Come back!" Immediately he could again sense the presence of the evil spirit.

Boldly he commanded, "Put it back!" When he did, the bed instantly slammed up against the wall!

"Now, leave!" the missionary commanded. And it did!

This missionary knew how to answer! Because he knew how to answer, the devil had to put back what he touched.

You have that same authority! What the devil has touched and stolen out of your life, command him, "Put it back!"

God delights in seeing to it that what the devil steals has to be put back!

Proverbs 6:31 declares that if a thief is found out, he has to restore sevenfold. Well, Jesus exposed Satan as the thief. So, since he has been found out, we have the right to demand that what he stole has to be restored back to us – in multiplied form! That's how to answer the thief!

Chapter 5

The Rewards of Answering Right

Most are well acquainted with the story of David and Goliath in 1 Samuel 17. Goliath was a Philistine who taunted God's people in battle. This giant's challenge to them was to send out one man to fight him. If the Israeli soldier killed Goliath, then the Philistines would become Israel's slaves. But if Goliath killed the Israeli, then Israel would become slaves to the Philistines. The outcome of one man's fight would affect the entire nation.

The men of Israel were so frightened to fight this giant that the entire army hid themselves. But day after day, Goliath would come out to taunt the men of Israel and challenge them to send someone to fight him. But no one would – they all hid.

It was during one of these threats of Goliath that David arrived on the scene to bring food to his brothers and check on their welfare.

He was shocked to hear Goliath threaten and taunt God's people, so he went to King Saul to offer to fight the giant.

Of course, King Saul was hesitant to allow this youth to represent Israel in a battle with a giant. But David was confident in knowing that God would back him up in his fight against this enemy.

Don't Be Afraid of Sounds You Hear

1 SAMUEL 17:32-37 (AMPC)
32 David said to Saul, Let no man's heart fail because of this Philistine; your servant will go out and fight with him.
33 And Saul said to David, You are not able to go to fight against this Philistine. You are only an adolescent, and he has been a warrior from his youth.
34 And David said to Saul, Your servant kept his father's sheep. And when there came a lion or again a bear and took a lamb out of the flock,
35 I went out after it and smote it and delivered the lamb out of its mouth; and when it arose against me, I caught it by its beard and smote it and killed it.
36 Your servant killed both the lion and the bear; and this uncircumcised Philistine shall be like one of them, for he has defied the armies of the living God!
37 David said, The Lord Who delivered me out of the paw of the lion and out of the paw of the bear, He will deliver me out of the hand of this Philistine. And Saul said to David, Go, and the Lord be with you!

David had much experience in standing his ground against enemies while protecting his father's sheep. He had fought deadly animals in keeping his father's sheep safe, but he had also spent long hours in the shepherd's field worshipping God, getting to know the God of his covenant.

In that shepherd's field, he had heard the sounds of the field in the heat of the day and in the dark of the night – lions, bears, and other wildlife. He had heard their sounds and had faced them unafraid.

The taunts of this giant were just another sound – a sound that he refused to be afraid of. He had already had experiences of winning against the sounds of his enemies.

You're going to hear many sounds in life from situations and circumstances, as well as from the devil. Don't be afraid of the sounds you hear. Don't fear them – answer them!

The Indignant Giant

King Saul finally agreed to let David fight Goliath, and he tried to get him to wear his armor. David refused, since he had no experience wearing armor, but instead, he took his slingshot as his weapon against the giant.

When Goliath saw David coming to the battlefield to answer his challenge, he was indignant that a youth would be sent to fight him, a man of war. The giant threatened David, *"Come to me, and I will give thy flesh unto the fowls of the air, and to the beasts of the field"* (1 Sam. 17:44).

But David not only knew how to use his slingshot – he knew how to answer!

> **1 SAMUEL 17:45-47**
> **45 Then said David to the Philistine, Thou comest to me with a sword, and with a spear, and with a shield: but I come to thee in the name of the Lord of hosts, the God of the armies of Israel, whom thou hast defied.**
> **46 This day will the Lord deliver thee into mine hand; and I will smite thee, and take thine head from thee; and I will give the carcases of the host of the Philistines this day unto the fowls of the air, and to the wild beasts of the earth; that all the earth may know that there is a God in Israel.**
> **47 And all this assembly shall know that the Lord saveth not with sword and spear: for the battle is the Lord's, and he will give you into our hands.**

Then after David answered, he took off running toward the giant. Before you move to deal with any difficulty in your way, answer it first. Answer in line with the Word, and Heaven will back you up.

The biggest thing that Goliath had on his side was himself, but David knew that he had the God of his covenant fighting for him. The men of Israel saw how big Goliath was, and they hid. David saw how big Goliath was, and he knew that he couldn't miss – and he didn't! The rock from his slingshot landed in Goliath's head; he fell to the ground, and then David took Goliath's sword and cut off his head.

Don't Listen to Your Enemy

When Goliath taunted the men of Israel, none of them answered him – they hid. They hid because they had listened to their enemy's threats day after day, and they believed him.

The devil may threaten you day after day, and if you listen long enough, you'll retreat instead of answering him. But don't believe him – answer him!

Romans 10:17 tells us, *"So then faith cometh by hearing, and hearing by the word of God."* The more you hear it, the more you'll believe it.

The devil knows this truth, too, so he will repeatedly speak something to try to get people to believe what he says. If you listen to the wrong thing long enough, you'll start believing the wrong thing. But remember, repetition doesn't make it true.

You can't keep the devil from talking, but you can keep from listening to and believing him. How? By answering him! Every time he talks, you have something to say! When fear says something to you, answer back! When symptoms speak to you, answer back! When circumstances threaten you, answer back! When old addictions rise up, answer back! When bad habits try to trip you up, answer back!

David was the only one who knew how to answer Goliath. He certainly wasn't the strongest or the most trained in battle, but he had spent enough time with God to know the answer to the threat of his enemies.

Focus on the Reward

When David said he would fight Goliath, he asked, "What's the reward for the man who defeats Goliath?" The reward was threefold: the king would give him great riches, the king would give him his daughter, and the man and his father's house would be free from taxes and service (1 Sam. 17:25, AMPC).

Let's look at each of these rewards. First, the king would give him great riches. Defeating Goliath would bring the victor great wealth. His place of opposition would become his wealthy place.

Answering your enemy and overcoming him will enrich you – it can become your wealthy place.

The second reward was that the victor would receive the king's daughter in marriage. In a moment, the victor would leave the ranks of a common man and come into union with royalty, in line for the throne. Then the children born to him would be of a royal bloodline.

The third reward was that the victor's father's house would be free from paying taxes and from having to serve in the military. Goliath wasn't just a giant – he was also a giant tax deduction!

So when David saw Goliath, he didn't focus on a great giant, but he focused on the great reward that awaited the victor – great wealth, marriage into the royal family, and tax-free living for himself and his family.

For the one who answers the giants in his life, there are rewards of answering right – a life of "more" awaits you. Don't focus on the giants in front of you, but focus on the rewards that await you on the other side of your right answers.

Your Answer Affects Others

Because David knew the answer and spoke it, he rescued a nation, his own family, and future generations. Whether or not you answer enemies, tests, and temptations right doesn't just affect you, but it affects others – your family and future generations.

Chapter 6

Keep It Behind You

Jesus spoke clearly and definitely to His disciples about what He would suffer at the hands of the religious leaders, but He also told them that He would be raised from the dead. Upon hearing these things, Peter considered this something that was to be fought against instead of God's plan that was to be fulfilled. So, in Matthew 16:22, Peter pulled Jesus aside and began to rebuke Him, saying, *"God forbid, Lord! This must never happen to You!"*

Verse 23 gives Jesus' response: *"But Jesus turned away from Peter and said to him, Get behind Me, Satan! You are in My way [an offense and a hindrance and a snare to Me]; for you are minding what partakes not of the nature and quality of God, but of men"* (AMPC).

Notice how Jesus not only rebuked Peter with His words, but His rebuke involved acting it out with His body – He turned His whole body away from Peter – He turned His back to Peter as He rebuked him.

When we answer the devil and circumstances, we can't be half-hearted or indefinite in our position. Once we answer opposition, every part of us must turn away from our opponent. We must not entertain or allow in the least degree any part of our attention to go or stay in the direction of our opposition – we must be wholehearted in our answering of the enemy and in our immovable stance against him. That includes not allowing our attention to go toward anything of the opposition. That's how we "turn our backs" toward the opposition.

This wasn't the only time that Jesus demonstrated His firm stance against opposition in this way, but we also see this same approach when Jesus was faced with Satan's temptations in the wilderness. In one of the three recorded temptations that Jesus faced, the devil took Jesus up to a high mountain and showed Him all of the kingdoms of the world in a moment of time.

> **LUKE 4:6-8**
> **6   And the devil said unto him, All this power will I give thee, and the glory of them: for that is delivered unto me; and to whomsoever I will I give it.**
> **7   If thou therefore wilt worship me, all shall be thine.**
> **8   And Jesus answered and said unto him, GET THEE BEHIND ME, SATAN: for it is written, Thou shalt worship the Lord thy God, and him only shalt though serve.**

No doubt, Jesus did to Satan what He did to Peter – He physically turned His back to him when He said, "Get thee behind Me, Satan."

This is our example. What are we doing when turning our backs to temptation? We are refusing to *look* at what the devil offers or suggests. If the devil can't get our attention, he can't get our future.

Where your attention goes, your faith goes. Refuse to allow your attention to go in the wrong direction, and you will keep the door closed to the wrong thing.

Temptations, the devil's threats, and wrong circumstances only belong in one place – behind you! Refuse to let them in front of you – keep them behind you! Answer them, then turn your back to them – turn your attention away from them.

Chapter 7

Don't Believe Everything You Feel

When the devil opposes, attacks, or threatens us, he also sends an influence that can be felt to try to persuade us to believe his threats.

There's nothing original in the devil because there's no life in him, only death; therefore, he can't author or create anything original. All he can do is imitate how God works, but he imitates with distortion.

When God speaks to us, we can sense His Presence and His anointing, which helps us to accept it as coming from Him. So, the devil does the same thing, only with distortion.

The devil suggests, tempts, or threatens us with something and also sends an influence that can be sensed or even felt to try to persuade us to accept it.

For example, the devil may suggest that you're going to lose your home, your job, or a loved one. When he threatens that, fear may try to grip you. Those words can feel so real to you – you can feel like what he threatens is true. That's an influence that he sends to try to get you to accept what he says.

But just because you can sense it or feel it doesn't make it true!

No matter what you may feel, answer it! Answer it with what the Word says. Resist it! Even if the feeling lingers, don't accept the wrong thoughts and threats just because you feel the wrong thing, no matter how long you may feel it. We walk by faith, by what we believe – not by what we feel or see.

"My Spirit's Not Shaking!"

I love the story one minister told. The devil had threatened him that a certain bad thing was going to happen. In the heat of this test, the devil said to him, "Now I've got you! You're afraid! Your body is shaking!"

The minister looked down to see his hands physically shaking – the fear was so tangible in the room. Then the minister answered, "Devil, my hands may be shaking, but that's not the 'real me.' The 'real me' is my spirit, and my spirit's not shaking!" With that, the devil left, and so did that influence of fear. That minister answered fear, and fear left!

Healing Is Still Yours

It's the same thing with physical symptoms. Just because you can feel symptoms in your body doesn't mean that healing no longer belongs to you. Healing is still yours, because Jesus paid the price for your healing, no matter what your body feels.

Refuse to change what you believe just because of what you feel. Keep believing that you are "the healed," no matter what you feel. Answer it!

What Are You Believing?

What you are believing is what you are believing *for!* So, make sure you are believing the right thing!

There were four different seasons in my life when I faced great attacks on my mind. With each test, I gained greater skill with the Word in standing my ground. I didn't realize it at the time, but these tests came at strategic times – when I was advancing into the next places of ministry God had for me. The enemy tries to oppose our advancements in the plan of God.

There was a pattern of one of these tests coming every 10 years. So, in the back of my mind I was counting down to the next 10-year mark.

One day, as I was considering this, God spoke to me, "Tests will come, but you don't have to *enter* them. You have the skill to not enter another test like that again, but if you think you have to, you will!" I was believing the wrong thing without realizing it.

If we aren't careful, we can let experiences of the past affect what we are believing.

I knew what God meant when He said that I had the skill to not enter the test. Because of having faced these tests, I had gained skill with my faith in the Word. I had learned how to stand in faith on God's Word and be untroubled in my mind by what opposed me and threatened me.

Victory is not the devil leaving you alone, but victory is learning to be completely untroubled by any devil or opposition that comes. Skillful faith answers opposition, then refuses to give it further notice or attention, for it's fixed on God and His Word.

Chapter 8

Words – A Living Force

Several years ago, I was working on a project that I believed would be a blessing to many people. About two weeks before it was completed, I heard the Spirit of God say to me, "You don't think that anything with the anointing on it is going to be unopposed, do you?" That let me know that opposition was coming.

The devil hates the anointing because it's the anointing that destroys the yoke that he tries to place on people and situations (Isa. 10:27). So anything with the anointing on it, he's going to oppose.

As we were completing the project one evening, I sensed an evil presence tangibly. When I sensed it, the devil said, "This project is going to fail! It will cost the ministry a lot of money, and it will bring great embarrassment to the ministry!" Those words were fiery darts that struck with force. A sense of fear tried to grip me, and those same words repeatedly circled my mind.

Have you ever seen a cartoon where a character hits someone else over the head and a halo of stars circle continuously around their head? That's how the enemy's words work. Wrong words are spoken to the mind, and once they're set in motion, they just keep circling around the head, looking for an entrance into the mind.

The words that spirit of fear spoke continually circled around my head, bringing great pressure against my mind as it tried to get in.

I had encountered the spirit of fear enough to learn how to keep from yielding to it. When I heard those words and sensed the fear, I spoke to that evil spirit, "Fear, you leave me in Jesus' Name." When I did, I sensed that spirit of fear stand back from me, but I also knew that it was still in the room.

I refused to let my attention go to it, but I still sensed its presence in the room, although it stood back.

I refused to be troubled by the fear that was present, so I went off to bed.

Because that fear followed at a distance, I had a bit of trouble falling asleep, but I eventually did. However, I was awakened several times with the words that the devil had spoken circling around my head. *This project is going to fail! It will cost the ministry a lot of money, and it will bring great embarrassment to the ministry!* Each time, I would just resist the spirit of fear and then go back to sleep.

As soon as I awoke early the next morning, the Spirit of God spoke to me. He said, "You answered the spirit of fear that spoke those words, and that's why he stood back. But you didn't answer the *words* that he spoke, and that's why those words are still moving, circling around your head, trying to get into your thought life. First, answer the *words*! Then answer the spirit that spoke the words, telling it to leave."

I saw it! The words that the spirit of fear spoke to me would keep circling and troubling my mind until *I stopped them*. How do you stop them? *Answer the words!* Speaking right words stops the movement of wrong words! You can't "out-think" wrong words – you have to answer them! Answer them with right words! I knew to answer the words *specifically*, not just *generally*. I didn't say, "I speak to those words to stop." I answered in line with what the words threatened. I said, "This project will not fail, but succeed! It will not bring financial loss to the ministry, and it will not bring great embarrassment to the ministry, but it will bless many people!"

When I answered those words specifically, they stopped! No more were the words that the devil spoke circling around my head, trying to get in and trouble my mind. Then I turned to that spirit of fear that spoke the words. It was still standing back in the room. I said, "Now, spirit of fear, leave me in Jesus' Name!" And it did! No more did it just stand back – it was gone!

I had learned a great lesson. The reason that the spirit of fear stood off initially without leaving when I first resisted it was because his words were still moving. Because his words were still moving, they gave him access. He was watching to see if I would take them into my thought life by turning them over in my mind. If I had, then he would have performed those words. He would have tried to cause the project to fail. But when I answered the words that he spoke, the words were aborted, so that spirit had no more access; therefore, he had to leave.

Words from the devil that we don't answer give him access, but when we immediately answer his words specifically, he can't gain access; his access is cut off.

We don't have to put up with long or short periods of time of mental harassment, torment, and bombardment. Answer those words and abort their movement. We don't need to keep praying about a problem that calls for us to answer it!

Jesus demonstrated that so masterfully to us when He was in the wilderness. He answered the words of the devil specifically.

Words Are a Living Force

Years ago, when I was very young in ministry, I had an experience that demonstrated the power of words. Every time that I would go to our offices, as soon as I would walk in, there would be a sense of heaviness or depression that would seem to hang over me like a cloud. Up until that time, I had always enjoyed being in the offices, but when this happened, I would get my work done as quickly as I could and get out of there. As soon as I walked out of the offices, that heaviness would leave me; that cloud would lift. I just thought that there was something wrong with me.

After about three months of this, I was in the office one day when it finally dawned on me that this wasn't just me, but this was being caused by something spiritual. So I got out of there and went home to pray. When I did, God spoke to me and showed me what to do. When I did what He showed me, we found out that someone in the offices had been repeatedly speaking against leadership. When we discovered that and dealt with it, that cloud, or heaviness, was gone.

If the negative words that people speak can have such a tangible effect and influence on you, the words that the devil and evil spirits speak can also influence you. But we are not their victim! We can stop the effect of those words by answering them!

The words you speak – good or bad – are living forces moving over people's lives. That's why it's so important that you speak the right words in your marriage, in your home, over your children, on the job, to fellow employees, and to everyone that you come in contact with.

Wrong words spoken in a home will change the entire atmosphere, charging it with strife and tension, robbing it of peace and joy. Wrong, harsh words spoken to or about a child will follow them like a dark cloud and affect everything about their thinking and their behavior. Wrong words spoken in a marriage will absolutely destroy that union.

But if wrong words spoken can have such a damaging, destructive effect, just think what right words will do to build, bless, and bring love, peace, and joy into a life and a home.

How do you stop and undo all the damage and destruction caused by wrong words? Speak right words. Speak love words. Speak God's Word. Answer the wrong words by replacing them with positive, loving, life-giving words.

If wrong words have been spoken against your life and are affecting you, you're not to be a victim of them. Answer them with the right words. Don't repeat or rehearse wrong words spoken to you. Just speak the right words, and they will dominate you and bless your life.

Words in Creation

The story of Creation in Genesis is a clear demonstration of the living force of words. Everything in Creation came about by words that God spoke. When He spoke, everything in Creation came into existence.

Words can create, or words can destroy. Choose your words wisely, for they are moving in your life and in the lives of others.

Chapter 9

Answer From Your Spirit

Years ago, I was going through a particular test that had lasted months and months. I was taking my stand on the Word and doing all that I knew to do, but I still didn't seem to be making progress; things weren't getting any better.

Finally, one day I said to the Lord, "I'm not sure if it's right to ask You for help regarding this because I know that it's my responsibility to exercise my authority over this opposition I'm facing and to stand my ground in faith. I'm endeavoring to do that as best as I know how. But things aren't changing – there's no progress. Now, I'm not asking You to do my part. But if there's something that You can do to help me with this, I'm asking You to help me." As I waited for a while before Him, I didn't hear Him say anything to me.

That night, I was leading a prayer meeting at our church. I had spent a short time teaching on prayer, then we began to pray. The moment that I closed my eyes to pray, I was instantly in the Spirit, and God spoke to me in response to my prayer earlier that day. He said, "It was right for you to ask Me to help you with what you're facing. Remember that when Paul was being buffeted, he prayed three times, asking

Me to help him with what he was facing, and I did. So, it was right for you to ask Me.

"No, I can't do your part, which is to stand your ground against the devil, but I can put you in the Spirit. Now that you're in the Spirit, speak to that evil spirit that has been harassing you and tell it to desist in its maneuvers against you."

So, I did. I said, "That evil spirit that has been harassing me, you desist in your maneuvers against me, in Jesus' Name!" And when I did, immediately I could tell the difference. And within a short time of that, every trace of that test that had been against me for months and months was completely over!

During the many months of the test, I had exercised my authority over the devil. I had told him to take his hands off of my life. But what was the difference? This time when I said it, I was in the Spirit!

It's not just the words that are spoken from the mental arena, from our mind, but words that are spoken from our spirit when we're in the Spirit. That makes all the difference!

Don't Be Drawn Into the Mental Arena

During a test, the devil will assault the mind with great force because he wants to draw us away from our spirit and into the mental arena. He tries to create so much commotion against our mind so that all of our attention will go to our mind and away from our spirit.

He knows that if he can hold us in the mental arena, he can whip us, and whip us badly, for the mental arena is his arena. He gains access into a person's life, even into a Christian's life, if they let him, through the mental arena.

But if we will hold him in the spirit arena, which is the faith arena, we will overcome him. Our faith is in our spirit, not our mind. That's why the devil wants to draw us away from our spirit, because then he is able to draw us out of faith.

He wants to draw us into the mental arena, trying to "figure out" how to get out of the test and overcome him. But we can't "figure out" how to get out of the test.

It's our job to stay out of the mental arena and stay in the spirit arena – the faith arena. For it's when we answer the devil and his lies from our spirit that the strategies he launches against our mind and life will fail.

Chapter 10

The Praise Flow

When the devil is trying to draw us into the mental arena and out of faith, he does it by bombarding the mind with troubling thoughts. How do we stay in the spirit arena and out of the mental arena when the mind is being bombarded?

First, answer those wrong thoughts with the Word. Then second, begin to praise. *Praising God helps hold you out of the mental arena and in the spirit arena, the faith arena.* Praise holds your attention on God and His Word and off of the enemy, off the test, and off the threats and suggestions he brings against the mind. Praising God helps to keep you from entertaining the thoughts of the enemy so that you don't turn wrong thoughts over and over in your mind.

Even if your praises seem dry at first, just keep praising. Depending on how long you've been entrenched in the mental arena, it may take a while, even a few days of focusing on praising the Lord, before your praises begin to flow out of your spirit, out of your heart.

But no matter how long it takes, keep praising. Get off by yourself as much as you can and praise God alone, as well as throughout the day. Refuse to let your mind run off in the wrong direction, but hold your attention on God and His Word. Focus on your spirit instead of your mind, and keep praising! Praise until you hit a note of victory.

Praising God brings the anointing, and it's the anointing that destroys the yoke.

Sometimes, there may be changes or corrections you must make to receive victory. If there's anything more that you need to know or do regarding your situation, as you are praising, you are in a position to hear what additional things He may say to you.

Praising God will help hold you in the Spirit. That's the arena where your victory flows from. So, praise your way into the victory flow – that's your flow!

As one minister said, "When you pray, you lay hold of things. But when you praise, you win battles!"

A Lifestyle of Praise & Worship

PSALM 9:1-3
1 I will praise thee, O Lord, with my whole heart; I will shew forth all thy marvellous works.
2 I will be glad and rejoice in thee: I will sing praise to thy name, O thou most High.
3 When mine enemies are turned back, they shall fall and perish at thy presence.

This passage tells us that when we praise God, we are to praise Him with our "whole heart." That means that our heart is to be engaged; we are not to just let praise become a meaningless action. When our heart is engaged, we get into the Presence of God and the anointing of God will begin flowing, and it's the anointing that destroys the yoke. In the Presence of God, our enemies fall. They are no match for the anointing of His Presence.

It's our job and privilege to stay in His Presence by keeping our heart and attention turned toward Him and His Word.

Psalm 34:1 instructs us, *"I will bless the Lord at ALL times: his praise shall CONTINUALLY be in my MOUTH."* Having a lifestyle of praising and worshipping God helps us to live in His Presence, and it helps us stay connected to our heart.

Praise is an act of faith, so praising continually holds us in a flow of faith continually. When praise is in our mouth, faith is in our mouth – our faith is being released – and the power of God meets faith.

His Presence

"When mine enemies are turned back, they shall fall and perish at thy presence" (Ps. 9:3).

One night, the enemy suggested all kinds of fearful scenarios to me. I refused to turn those thoughts and threats over in my mind, but answered them with the Word, then I began boldly praising God. However, while I was praising,

I was prompted to just be still and focus on and rest in the Presence of God. When I did, God spoke to me and gave me further revelation. When I acted on that revelation, that opposition was easily overcome.

When faced with opposition, or when nothing seems to be happening, we tend to push more, when sometimes we need to pull back – just be still and listen to Him. As we trust Him and rest in His Presence, He goes to work for us. Our enemies fall and perish at His Presence.

Years ago, my husband was called to minister to a woman who was in the hospital and facing surgery. This woman had a walk with God that was rich and rare; she was a lesson on living in God's Presence. When my husband and I came into her hospital room, she told us what the doctors had said about her condition, then she said, "But I just don't let my mind go there – I just stay in His Presence," and she laid back in the bed and worshipped. She was a picture of peace as she held her attention and focus on Him. She came through that situation easily and lived about another 30 years before she moved to Heaven.

On one occasion, someone had asked me to help them with a particular need, and God told me to do it, so I did. Afterwards, the devil repeatedly threatened me, "Now you have put yourself in a difficult place by doing that."

But I answered him, "No, devil, I never put myself in a difficult place by obeying God!"

Over and over, the enemy would say the same thing to me, and I would just answer him the same way. After about 30 minutes of this, God spoke to me, "If you would just live in My Presence, you wouldn't even have to listen to that!"

The problem wasn't that the enemy was speaking. The problem was that I wasn't "in the Spirit" as I should have been – my attention wasn't on God and His Presence as it should have been.

As we live in God's Presence, with our mind, attention, and praises fixed on Him, we are out of reach of the enemy's assaults that he launches. This is in keeping with Psalm 91:8, *"Only a spectator shall you be [yourself INACCESSIBLE in the secret place of the Most High]..."* (AMPC).

We experience uninterrupted peace and victory as we live in His Presence.

Chapter 11

Three Steps to Victory

When you're faced with opposition, the devil doesn't want you to think that your victory is simple, but it is. Situations and circumstances may look complicated or tangled to you, but just because a situation may be complicated, that doesn't mean that the answer is complicated – it's simple.

Reviewing the previous chapters, I want to highlight the three steps you are to take when tested:

1. Answer every wrong, troubling thought or threat specifically.

2. Tell the spirit that spoke the thought to leave in Jesus' Name – whether it's the spirit of fear, doubt, or unbelief. If fear comes, say, "Fear, I resist you." If doubt or unbelief comes, say, "Doubt, unbelief, I resist you."

3. Praise God continually – it will help you hold your attention and thoughts on God and off of the opposition.

   Praise brings the anointing, which destroys the yoke.

If there's anything more that you need to know
or do, as you praise, you are in a position to hear
Him.

The devil may tell you that your situation is so big that
these steps aren't enough and that they won't work. He
wants to get your mind involved, trying to find something
hard to do, but Jesus already did the hard part and gave us
the simple part.

Don't dismiss the answers given in this book. Doing the
Word always works. It's more than enough for every situation.

When you learn to answer every opposition, test,
temptation, and wrong or troubling thought, you become
more skillful with your authority, and you will enjoy the
victory that already belongs to you.

Prayer of Salvation

Heavenly Father, I come to You in the Name of Jesus. Your Word says, *"...him that cometh to me I will in no wise cast out"* (John 6:37). So I know You won't cast me out, but You will take me in, and I thank You for it.

You said in Your Word, *"...If thou shalt confess with thy mouth the Lord Jesus, and shalt believe in thine heart that God hath raised him from the dead, thou shalt be saved. For whosoever shall call upon the name of the Lord shall be saved"* (Rom. 10:9 & 13).

I believe in my heart that Jesus Christ is the Son of God. I believe Jesus died for my sins and was raised from the dead so I can be in right-standing with God. I am calling upon His Name, the Name of Jesus, so I know, Father, that You save me now.

Your Word says, *"...with the heart man believeth unto righteousness; and with the mouth confession is made unto salvation"* (Rom. 10:10). I do believe with my heart, and I confess Jesus now as my Lord. Therefore, I am saved! Thank You, Father.

Please write us and let us know that you have just been born again. When you write, ask to receive our salvation booklets.

To contact us, please email us at
dm@dufresneministries.org
or write to:
Dufresne Ministries
P.O. Box 1010
Murrieta, CA 92564

How To Be Filled With the Holy Spirit

Acts 2:38 reads, *"...Repent, and be baptized every one of you in the name of Jesus Christ for the remission of sins, and ye shall receive the GIFT of the Holy Ghost."* The Holy Ghost is a gift that belongs to each one of God's people. Jesus is the gift God gave the whole world, but the Holy Spirit is a gift that belongs only to God's people.

Jesus told His disciples, *"But ye shall receive POWER, after that the Holy Ghost is come upon you: and ye shall be witnesses unto me..."* (Acts 1:8). When you're baptized with the Holy Spirit, you receive supernatural power that enables you to live victoriously.

Indwelling vs. Infilling

When you're born again, you receive the indwelling of the Person of the Holy Spirit. Romans 8:16 tells us, *"The Spirit itself* (Himself) *beareth witness with our spirit, that we are the children of God."* When you're born again, you know it because the Spirit bears witness with your own spirit that you are a child of God; He confirms it to you. He's able to bear witness with your spirit because He's in you; you are *indwelt* by the Spirit of God.

But the Word of God speaks of another experience subsequent to the new birth that belongs to every believer, and that is to be baptized with the Holy Spirit, or to receive the *infilling* of the Holy Spirit.

God wants you to be full and overflowing with the Spirit. Being filled with the Spirit is likened to being full of water. Just because you had one drink of water doesn't mean you're full of water. At the new birth, you received the indwelling of the Spirit – a drink of water. But now God wants you to be filled to overflowing – be filled with His Spirit, baptized with the Holy Ghost.

> **ACTS 2:1-4**
> **1 And when the day of Pentecost was fully come, they were all with one accord in one place.**
> **2 And suddenly there came a sound from heaven as of a rushing mighty wind, and it filled all the house where they were sitting.**
> **3 And there appeared unto them cloven tongues like as of fire, and it sat upon each of them.**
> **4 And they were all FILLED with the Holy Ghost, and BEGAN TO SPEAK WITH OTHER TONGUES, as the Spirit gave them utterance.**

When these disciples were filled with the Holy Ghost, they began to speak with other tongues as the Spirit gave them utterance; they spoke in a language unknown to them. Today, when a believer is filled with the Holy Ghost, they will speak with other tongues too. These are not words that come from the mind of man, but they are words given by the Holy Spirit; these words float up from their spirit within, and the person then speaks those out.

What is the benefit of being filled with the Holy Ghost with the evidence of speaking in other tongues? First Corinthians 14:2 reads, *"For he that speaketh in an unknown tongue speaketh not unto men, but unto God...."* When you're speaking in other tongues, you're speaking to God – it is a divine means of communicating with your Heavenly Father. This is one of many great benefits.

> **MATTHEW 7:7-11**
> **7   Ask, and it shall be given you...**
> **8   FOR EVERY ONE THAT ASKETH RE-CEIVETH...**
> **9   ...what man is there of you, whom if his son ask bread, will he give him a stone?**
> **10 Or if he ask a fish, will he give him a serpent?**
> **11 If ye then, being evil, know how to give good gifts unto your children, HOW MUCH MORE SHALL YOUR FATHER WHICH IS IN HEAVEN GIVE GOOD THINGS TO THEM THAT ASK HIM?**

In this passage, Jesus is saying that when you ask God for something, you shall receive it! Believe that He will give you that which you ask for. When you ask God for something good, He won't give you something that will harm you; He will give you the good thing you ask for. The baptism of the Holy Spirit is a good gift, and when you ask God to fill you with the Holy Spirit, you won't receive a wrong spirit; you will receive this good gift, the gift of the Holy Spirit.

Once you receive the gift of the Holy Ghost, you can yield to this gift any time, speaking in other tongues as often as you choose; you don't have to wait for God to move on you. The more you speak in other tongues, the more you will benefit from this gift. By continuing to speak in other tongues on a daily basis, you will be able to maintain a Spirit-filled life; you will live full of the Spirit.

The more you take time to speak in other tongues, the deeper you'll move into the things of God.

(For more teaching on being filled with the Holy Spirit, I recommend the mini-book, *Why Tongues?* by Kenneth E. Hagin.)

Prayer To Receive
the Holy Spirit

"Father, I see that the gift of the Holy Spirit belongs to Your children. So, I come to You to receive this gift. I received my salvation by faith, so I receive the gift of the Holy Spirit by faith. I believe I receive the Holy Spirit now! Since I'm filled with the Holy Spirit now, I expect to speak in other tongues as the Spirit gives me utterance, just like those in Acts 2 on the Day of Pentecost. Thank You for filling me with the Holy Ghost."

Now, words that the Spirit of God gives you will float up from your spirit. You are the one who must open your mouth and speak those words out. The words will not come to your mind, but they will float up from your spirit. Speak those out freely.